Contents

KT-446-703

Acknowledgements

The publishers would like to thank Gray-Nicolls for their photographic contribution to this book.

Photographs on the front cover and pages 14, 30, 32, 34, 38, 41 and 42 courtesy of Sporting Pictures (UK) Ltd. Photographs on the inside front cover, pages 2, 46 and 47, the inside back cover and the back cover courtesy of Allsport UK Ltd. Photograph on page 39 courtesy of Empics Ltd.
Illustrations by Tim Bairstow of Taurus Graphics.

Note   Throughout the book players, umpires and scorers are referred to individually as 'he'. This should, of course, be taken to mean 'he or she' where appropriate.

1

Introduction

Since its formation in 1787, Marylebone Cricket Club (M.C.C.) has been recognised throughout the world as the sole authority for drawing up Codes of the Laws of Cricket and for all subsequent alterations. The latest Code was produced in 1980.

The Laws and Official Notes are given in full in this book, supplemented with additional comments based on the 1980 Code. While not being official in the strictest sense, it is believed that these comments represent the best opinion available on points which give rise to uncertainty in the minds of inexperienced players, umpires and scorers.

Umpires may wish to refer especially to the sections picked out in red; they have been selected by John Jameson, Assistant Secretary of M.C.C., in view of their particular importance.

The game

Cricket is played between two teams, normally 11 a side, and gives the maximum opportunity for combining team effort with individual skill and initiative. Each team bats, or takes its innings, in turn – the choice for first innings being decided by toss. The game is played on a pitch on which two wickets are placed 22 yards (20.12 m) apart, although this distance may be reduced for young children.

The two batsmen defend these wickets against the bowling of the fielding side, and when a batsman is 'out' his place is taken by another, and so on until ten batsmen are out or until the innings has been declared closed.

A bowler from the fielding side bowls an over of 6 balls from one end to the opposite batsman defending his wicket, and aims to dismiss the batsman in one of the ways provided for in the Laws.

The more common methods of dismissing a batsman are the bowling down of the striker's wicket, catching him from a stroke, his being Leg Before Wicket, stumping by the wicket-keeper when he has gone out of his ground, and the running out of either batsman while attempting a run.

Overs are bowled successively from alternate ends. No bowler can bowl two overs in succession, but with that restriction the captain of the fielding side can change his bowling as he thinks fit.

The score is reckoned by 'runs', i.e. the number of times the batsmen run from end to end of the area between the 'popping crease' at each end of the pitch. Runs are usually the result of hits, but can be scored when the ball has not actually been hit by the striker, e.g. 'byes' and 'leg-byes', or as penalties for 'wides' and 'no balls'. The fielding side has the twofold object of dismissing the opposing batsmen and of preventing them from scoring runs.

When the first side has completed its innings, the other side starts its own. A match may consist of one or two innings by each side. The side scoring the largest aggregate of runs in the match is the winner. If the match is not played out to a finish, it is regarded as drawn.

The laws

Law 1 – the players

1. Number of players and captain
A match is played between two sides each of 11 players, one of whom shall be captain. In the event of the captain not being available at any time a deputy shall act for him.

2. Nomination of players
Before the toss for innings, the captain shall nominate his players who may not thereafter be changed without the consent of the opposing captain.

Notes
a More or less than 11 players a side: *a match may be played by agreement between sides of more or less than 11 players but not more than 11 players may field.*

Law 2 – substitutes and runners: batsman or fieldsman leaving the field: batsman retiring: batsman commencing innings

1. Substitutes
In normal circumstances, a substitute shall be allowed to field only for a player who satisfies the umpires that he has become injured or become ill during the match. However, in very exceptional circumstances, the umpires may use their discretion to allow a substitute for a player who has to leave the field for other wholly acceptable reasons, subject to consent being given by the opposing captain. If a player wishes to change his shirt, boots, etc., he may leave the field to do so (no changing on the field) but no substitute will be allowed.

2. Objection to substitutes
The opposing captain shall have no right of objection to any player acting as substitute on the field, nor as to where he shall field; however, no substitute shall act as wicket-keeper.

3. Substitute not to bat or bowl
A substitute shall not be allowed to bat or bowl.

4. A player for whom a substitute has acted
A player may bat, bowl or field even though a substitute has acted for him.

5. Runner
A runner shall be allowed for a batsman who during the match is incapacitated by illness or injury. The player acting as runner shall be a member of the batting side and shall, if possible, have already batted in that innings.

6. Runner's equipment
The player acting as runner for an injured batsman shall wear the same external protective equipment as the injured batsman.

7. Transgression of the laws by an injured batsman or runner
An injured batsman may be out should his runner break any one of Laws 33 (Handled the ball), 37 (Obstructing the field) or 38 (Run out). As striker he remains himself subject to the Laws.

Furthermore, should he be out of his ground for any purpose and the wicket at the wicket-keeper's end be put down he shall be out under Law 38 (Run out) or Law 39 (Stumped) irrespective of the position of the other batsman or the runner and no runs shall be scored.

When not the striker, the injured batsman is out of the game and shall stand where he does not interfere with the play. Should he bring himself into the game in any way then he shall suffer the penalties that any transgression of the Laws demands.

8. Fieldsman leaving the field
No fieldsman shall leave the field or return during a session of play without the consent of the umpire at the bowler's end. The umpire's consent is also necessary if a substitute is required for a fieldsman, when his side returns to the field after an interval. If a member of the fielding side leaves the field or fails to return after an interval and is absent from the field for longer than 15 minutes, he shall not be permitted to bowl after his return until he has been on the field for at least that length of playing time for which he was absent.

This restriction shall not apply at the start of a new day's play.

9. Batsman leaving the field or retiring

A batsman may leave the field or retire at any time owing to illness, injury or other unavoidable cause, having previously notified the umpire at the bowler's end. He may resume his innings at the fall of a wicket, which for the purposes of this Law shall include the retirement of another batsman.

If he leaves the field or retires for any other reason he may only resume his innings with the consent of the opposing captain.

When a batsman has left the field or retired and is unable to return owing to illness, injury or other unavoidable cause, his innings is to be recorded as 'retired, not out'. Otherwise it is to be recorded as 'retired, out'.

10. Commencement of a batsman's innings

A batsman shall be considered to have commenced his innings once he has stepped on to the field of play.

Notes

a Substitutes and runners: *for the purpose of these Laws allowable illnesses or injuries are those which occur at any time after the nomination by the captains of their teams.*

Comments

Notice particularly that a substitute can only be claimed as a right for a player who becomes unfit during the match. In all other cases consent of the opposing captain is necessary.

Law 2.4 is important: it means that a player on the team list can bat, even if a substitute has fielded for him throughout an innings. Note also that the Law does not prevent a substitute from keeping wicket, although the opposing captain has the right to object to this.

If an injured batsman, when not the striker, brings himself into the game in any way, he must suffer the penalties that any transgression of the Laws demands.

Law 3 – the umpires

1. Appointment

Before the toss for innings two umpires shall be appointed, one for each end, to control the game with absolute impartiality as required by the Laws.

2. Change of umpire

No umpire shall be changed during a match without the consent of both captains.

3. Special conditions

Before the toss for innings, the umpires shall agree with both captains on any special conditions affecting the conduct of the match.

4. The wickets

The umpires shall satisfy themselves before the start of the match that the wickets are properly pitched.

5. Clock or watch

The umpires shall agree between themselves and inform both captains before the start of the match on the watch or clock to be followed during the match.

6. Conduct and implements

Before and during a match the umpires shall ensure that the conduct of the game and the implements used are strictly in accordance with the Laws.

7. Fair and unfair play

The umpires shall be the sole judges of fair and unfair play.

8. Fitness of ground, weather and light

a The umpires shall be the sole judges of the fitness of the ground, weather and light for play.

(i) However, before deciding to suspend play or not to start play or not to resume play after an interval or stoppage, the umpires shall establish whether both captains (the batsmen at the wicket may deputise for their captain) wish to commence or to continue in the prevailing conditions; if so, their wishes shall be met.

(ii) In addition, if during play the umpires decide that the light is unfit, only the batting side shall have the option of continuing play. After agreeing to continue to play in unfit light conditions, the captain of the batting side (or a batsman at the wicket) may appeal against the light to the umpires, who shall uphold the appeal only if, in their opinion, the light has deteriorated since the agreement to continue was made.

b After any suspension of play, the umpires, unaccompanied by any of the players or officials, shall, on their own initiative, carry out an inspection immediately the conditions improve and shall continue to inspect at intervals. Immediately the umpires decide that play is possible they shall call upon the players to resume the game.

9. Exceptional circumstances

In exceptional circumstances, other than those of weather, ground or light, the umpires may decide to suspend or abandon play. Before making such a decision the umpires shall establish, if the circumstances allow, whether both captains (the batsmen at the wicket may deputise for their captain) wish to continue in the prevailing conditions: if so their wishes shall be met.

10. Position of umpires

The umpires shall stand where they can best see any act upon which their decision may be required.

Subject to this over-riding consideration the umpire at the bowler's end shall stand where he does not interfere with either the bowler's run-up or the striker's view.

The umpire at the striker's end may elect to stand on the off instead of the leg side of the pitch, provided he informs the captain of the fielding side and the striker of his intention to do so.

11. Umpires changing ends

The umpires shall change ends after each side has had one innings.

12. Disputes

All disputes shall be determined by the umpires and if they disagree the actual state of things shall continue.

13. Signals

The following code of signals shall be used by umpires who will wait until a signal has been answered by a scorer before allowing the game to proceed.

Boundary 4 – by waving the arm from side to side.
Boundary 6 – by raising both arms above the head.

Fig. 1 Umpire's signals: (a) boundary 4; ▶
(b) boundary 6; (c) bye; (d) dead ball;
(e) leg-bye; (f) no ball; (g) calling no ball;
(h) out; (i) short run; (j) wide ball

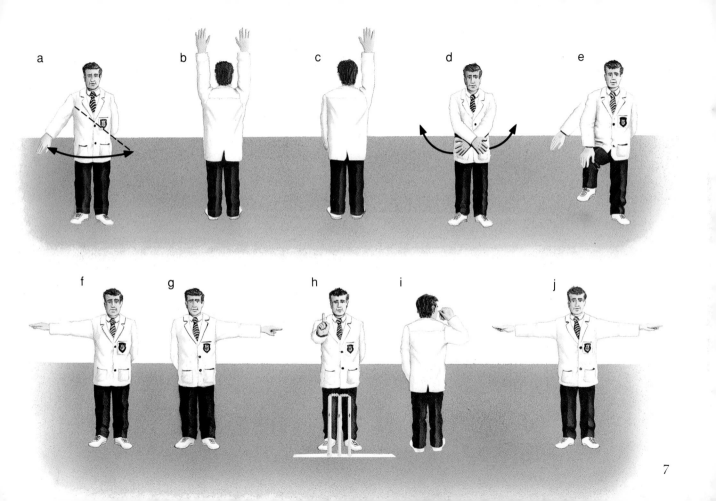

7

Bye	– by raising an open hand above the head.
Dead ball	– by crossing and recrossing the wrists below the waist.
Leg-bye	– by touching a raised knee with the hand.
No ball	– by extending one arm horizontally.
Out	– by raising the index finger above the head. If not out the umpire shall call 'not out'.
Short run	– by bending the arm upwards and by touching the nearer shoulder with the tips of the fingers.
Wide	– by extending both arms horizontally.

14. Correctness of scores

The umpires shall be responsible for satisfying themselves on the correctness of the scores throughout and at the conclusion of the match. *See* Law 21.6 (Correctness of result).

Notes

a Attendance of umpires: *the umpires should be present on the ground and report to the ground executive or the equivalent at least 30 minutes before the start of a day's play.*

b Consultation between umpires and scorers: *consultation between umpires and scorers over doubtful points is essential.*

c Fitness of ground: *the umpires shall consider the ground as unfit for play when it is so wet or slippery as to deprive the bowlers of a reasonable foothold, the fieldsmen, other than the deep-fielders, of the power of free movement, or the batsmen the ability to play their strokes or to run between the wickets. Play should not be suspended merely because the grass and the ball are wet and slippery.*

d Fitness of weather and light: *the umpires should only suspend play when they consider that the conditions are so bad that it is unreasonable or dangerous to continue.*

Comments

If in a one or half-day match the innings are restricted by time or a specified number of overs, it is essential for the umpires to ensure that both captains are clear as to the agreed conditions.

With reference to Law 3.10, it is clearly in the interest of the fielders that the umpire's view is unobstructed. They will therefore seldom be wise to press the umpire to stand where he does not want to; they can never insist on his doing so.

An umpire is not required to inform an incoming batsman of the number of balls remaining in the 'over' in progress, but he should give the information if asked for it. An umpire should not call 'Last over' before any interval or close of play.

In a one-day match the umpires do not change ends before each side has completed an innings.

With reference to laws 3.7 and 42.2, while the wearing of gloves by the wicket-keeper is an understood practice, fielders should not wear gloves, bandages or plaster to protect their hands without the consent of the opposing captain, and then only if special circumstances necessitate it. The umpires should enquire if permission has been granted in such cases.

With reference to Law 3.8, note that play should only be suspended if conditions are so bad that it is dangerous or unreasonable to continue.

Law 4 – the scorers

1. Recording runs

All runs scored shall be recorded by scorers appointed for the purpose. Where there are two scorers they shall frequently check to ensure that the score sheets agree.

2. Acknowledging signals

The scorers shall accept and immediately acknowledge all instructions and signals given to them by the umpires.

Comments

Although the scorers cannot dictate to the umpires, they are entitled to question them on any point about which doubt exists. Particularly in practice games played by juniors, they may also call the attention of the umpires to such points as persistent miscounting of the number of balls in the 'over', but play should not normally be interrupted for this purpose.

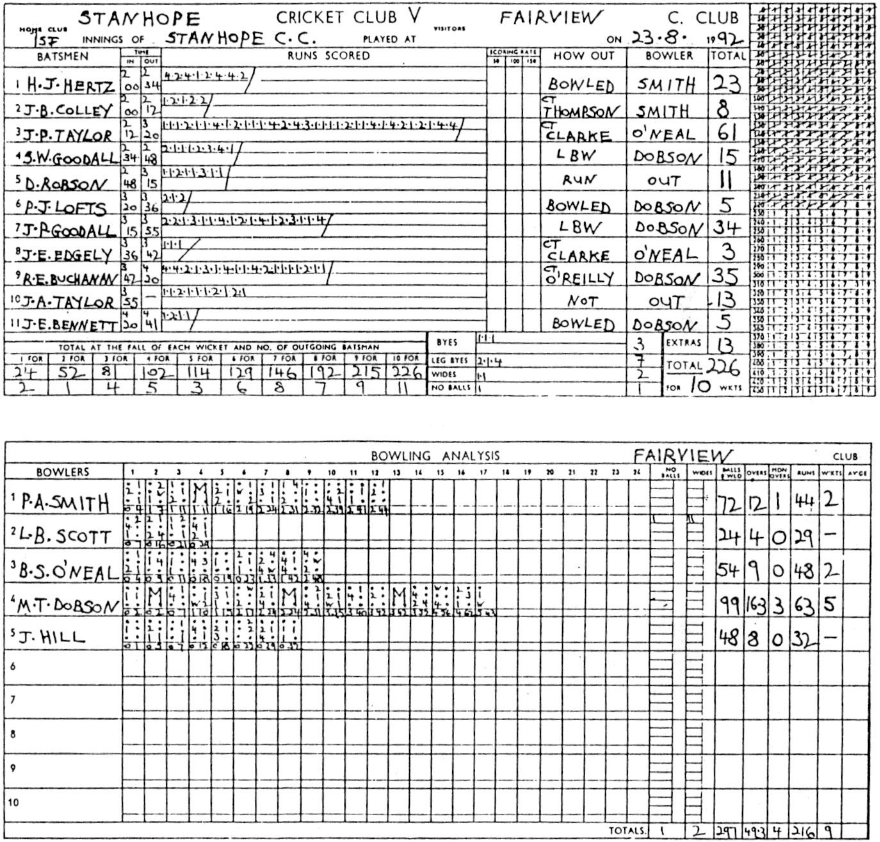

Fig. 2 A typical score sheet and bowling analysis ▶

STANHOPE CRICKET CLUB V FAIRVIEW C. CLUB
HOME CLUB — 1ST INNINGS OF STANHOPE C.C. — PLAYED AT — on 23·8·1992

BATSMEN	HOW OUT	BOWLER	TOTAL
1 H·J·HERTZ	BOWLED	SMITH	23
2 J·B·COLLEY	CT THOMPSON	SMITH	8
3 J·P·TAYLOR	CT CLARKE	O'NEAL	61
4 S·W·GOODALL	LBW	DOBSON	15
5 D·ROBSON	RUN OUT		11
6 P·J·LOFTS	BOWLED	DOBSON	5
7 J·R·GOODALL	LBW	DOBSON	34
8 J·E·EDGELY	CT CLARKE	O'NEAL	3
9 R·E·BUCHANAN	CT O'REILLY	DOBSON	35
10 J·A·TAYLOR	NOT OUT		13
11 J·E·BENNETT	BOWLED	DOBSON	5

Extras: BYES 3, LEG BYES 2·1·4 = 7, WIDES 1, NO BALLS 1 — EXTRAS 13
TOTAL 226 for 10 WKTS

TOTAL AT THE FALL OF EACH WICKET AND NO. OF OUTGOING BATSMAN

1 FOR	2 FOR	3 FOR	4 FOR	5 FOR	6 FOR	7 FOR	8 FOR	9 FOR	10 FOR
24	52	81	102	114	129	146	192	215	226
2	1	4	5	3	6	8	7	9	11

BOWLING ANALYSIS — FAIRVIEW CLUB

BOWLERS	BALLS	MAIDENS	NO BALLS	RUNS	WKTS	AVGE
1 P·A·SMITH	72	12	1	44	2	
2 L·B·SCOTT	24	4	0	29	–	
3 B·S·O'NEAL	54	9	0	48	2	
4 M·T·DOBSON	99	16	3	3 65	5	
5 J·HILL	48	8	0	32	–	

TOTALS: 1 2 297 49 3 4 216 9

9

Law 5 – the ball

1. Weight and size
The ball, when new, shall weigh not less than $5\frac{1}{2}$ ounces/155.9 g, nor more than $5\frac{3}{4}$ ounces/163 g; and shall measure not less than $8\frac{13}{16}$ inches/22.4 cm, nor more than 9 inches/22.9 cm in circumference.

2. Approval of balls
All balls used in matches shall be approved by the umpires and captains before the start of a match.

▲ *A cricket ball's weight shall be $5\frac{1}{2}$–$5\frac{3}{4}$ ounces (155.9–163 g). Its circumference shall be $8\frac{13}{16}$–9 inches (22.4–22.9 cm)*

3. New ball
Subject to agreement to the contrary, having been made before the toss, either captain may demand a new ball at the start of each innings.

4. New ball in match of 3 or more days' duration
In a match of 3 or more days' duration, the captain of the fielding side may demand a new ball after the prescribed number of overs has been bowled with the old one. The governing body for cricket in the country concerned shall decide the number of overs applicable in that country which shall be not less than 75 6-ball overs.

5. Ball lost or becoming unfit for play
In the event of a ball during play being lost or, in the opinion of the umpires, becoming unfit for play, the umpires shall allow it to be replaced by one that in their opinion has had a similar amount of wear. If a ball is to be replaced, the umpires shall inform the batsmen.

Notes

a Specifications: *the specifications, as described in* **1** *above shall apply to top-grade balls only. The following degrees of tolerance will be acceptable for other grades of ball.*
(i) Men's grades 2–4
Weight: $5\frac{5}{16}$ ounces/150 g to $5\frac{13}{16}$ ounces/ 165 g. Size: $8\frac{11}{16}$ inches/22.0 cm to $9\frac{1}{16}$ inches/23.0 cm.
(ii) Women's
Weight: $4\frac{15}{16}$ ounces/140 g to $5\frac{5}{16}$ ounces/ 150 g. Size: $8\frac{1}{4}$ inches/21.0 cm to $8\frac{7}{8}$ inches/22.5 cm.
(iii) Junior
Weight: $4\frac{5}{16}$ ounces/133 g to $5\frac{1}{16}$ ounces/ 143 g. Size: $8\frac{1}{16}$ inches/20.5 cm to $8\frac{11}{16}$ inches/22.0 cm.

Law 6 – the bat

1. Width and length
The bat overall shall not be more than 38 inches/96.5 cm in length; the blade of the bat shall be made of wood and shall not exceed $4\frac{1}{4}$ inches/10.8 cm at the widest part.

Notes

a The blade of the bat may be covered with material for protection, strengthening or repair. Such material shall not exceed $\frac{1}{16}$ inch/1.56 mm in thickness.

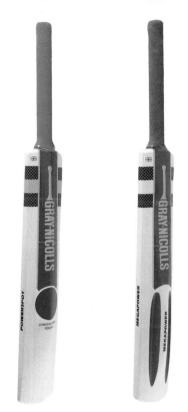

▲ *A cricket bat shall be no more than 38 inches (96.5 cm) in length and no more than $4\frac{1}{4}$ inches (10.8 cm) in width*

▲ *Batsman's protective gloves*

▼ *Batsman's protective legguards*

Comments

A child's batting may be seriously handicapped by use of too large or too heavy a bat.

▲ *It is customary for cricket players to wear predominantly white clothing and footwear*

Law 7 – the pitch

1. Area of pitch
The pitch is the area between the bowling creases – *see* Law 9 (The bowling, popping and return creases). It shall measure 5 ft/1.52 m in width on either side of a line joining the centre of the middle stumps of the wickets – *see* Law 8 (The wickets).

2. Selection and preparation
Before the toss for innings, the executive of the ground shall be responsible for the selection and preparation of the pitch; thereafter the umpires shall control its use and maintenance.

3. Changing pitch
The pitch shall not be changed during a match unless it becomes unfit for play, and then only with the consent of both captains.

4. Non-turf pitches
In the event of a non-turf pitch being used, the following shall apply.

a Length: that of the playing surface to a minimum of 58 ft (17.68 m).
b Width: that of the playing surface to a minimum of 6 ft (1.83 m).

See Law 10 (Rolling, sweeping, mowing, watering the pitch and re-marking of creases) *Note* **a**.

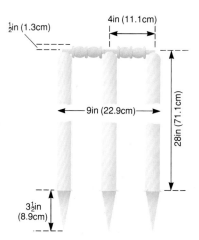

▲ *Fig. 3 Dimensions of stumps and bails*

Law 8 – the wickets

1. Width and pitching
Two sets of wickets, each 9 inches/22.86 cm wide, and consisting of three wooden stumps with two wooden bails upon the top, shall be pitched opposite and parallel to each other at a distance of 22 yards/20.12 m between the centres of the two middle stumps.

2. Size of stumps
The stumps shall be of equal and sufficient size to prevent the ball from passing between them. Their tops shall be 28 inches/71.1 cm above the ground, and shall be dome-shaped except for the bail grooves.

3. Size of bails
The bails shall be each $4\frac{3}{8}$ inches/11.1 cm in length and when in position on the top of the stumps shall not project more than $\frac{1}{2}$ inch/1.3 cm above them.

Notes
a Dispensing with bails: *in a high wind the umpires may decide to dispense with the use of bails.*

b Junior cricket: *for junior cricket, as defined by the local governing body, the following measurements for the wickets shall apply.*

Width – *8 inches/20.32 cm.*
Pitched – *21 yards/19.20 m.*
Height – *27 inches/68.58 cm.*
Bails – *each $3\frac{7}{8}$ inches/9.84 cm in length and should not project more than $\frac{1}{2}$ inch/1.3 cm above them.*

Law 9 – the bowling, popping and return creases

1. The bowling crease
The bowling crease shall be marked in line with the stumps at each end and shall be 8 ft 8 inches/2.64 m in length, with the stumps in the centre.

2. The popping crease
The popping crease, which is the back edge of the crease marking, shall be in front of and parallel with the bowling crease. It shall have the back edge of the crease marking 4 ft/1.22 m from the centre of the stumps and shall extend to a minimum of 6 ft/1.83 m on either side of the line of the wicket.

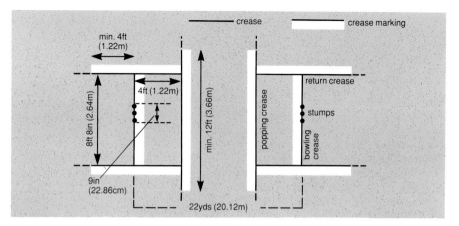

▲ *Fig. 4 Dimensions of pitch, wickets and creases*

The popping crease shall be considered to be unlimited in length.

3. The return crease
The return crease marking, of which the inside edge is the crease, shall be at each end of the bowling crease and at right angles to it. The return crease shall be marked to a minimum of 4 ft/1.22 m behind the wicket and shall be considered to be unlimited in length. A forward extension shall be marked to the popping crease.

Comments
To be within his ground a batsman must have some part of his bat or person grounded inside the popping crease. (*See* Law 29.)

Law 10 – rolling, sweeping, mowing, watering the pitch and re-marking of creases

1. Rolling
During the match the pitch may be

13

rolled at the request of the captain of the batting side, for a period of not more than 7 minutes before the start of each innings, other than the first innings of the match, and before the start of each day's play. In addition, if, after the toss and before the first innings of the match, the start is delayed, the captain of the batting side may request to have the pitch rolled for not more than 7 minutes. However, if in the opinion of the umpires, the delay has had no significant effect upon the state of the pitch, they shall refuse any request for the rolling of the pitch.

The pitch shall not otherwise be rolled during the match.

The 7 minutes rolling permitted before the start of a day's play shall take place not earlier than half an hour before the start of play and the captain of the batting side may delay such rolling until 10 minutes before the start of play should he so desire.

If a captain declares an innings closed less than 15 minutes before the resumption of play, and the other captain is thereby prevented from exercising his option of 7 minutes rolling or if he is so prevented for any other reason the time for rolling shall be taken out of the normal playing time.

2. Sweeping
Such sweeping of the pitch as is necessary during the match shall be done so that the 7 minutes allowed for rolling the pitch provided for in **1** above is not affected.

3. Mowing
a Responsibilities of ground authority and of umpires: all mowings which are carried out before the toss for innings shall be the responsibility of the ground authority. Thereafter they shall be carried out under the supervision of the umpires, *see* Law 7.2 (Selection and preparation).

▲ *The pitch may be swept if necessary. Creases shall be re-marked whenever possible*

b Initial mowing: the pitch shall be mown before play begins on the day the match is scheduled to start or in the case of a delayed start on the day the match is expected to start. *See* **a** above (Responsibilities of ground authority and of umpires).

c Subsequent mowings in a match of 2 or more days' duration: in a match of 2 or more day's duration, the pitch shall be mown daily before play begins. Should this mowing not take place because of weather conditions, rest days or other reasons the pitch shall be mown on the first day on which the match is resumed.

d Mowing of the outfield in a match of 2 or more days' duration: in order to ensure that conditions are as similar as possible for both sides, the outfield shall normally be mown before the commencement of play on each day of the match, if ground and weather conditions allow. *See Note* **b** to this Law.

4. Watering
The pitch shall not be watered during a match.

5. Re-marking creases
Whenever possible the creases shall be re-marked.

6. Maintenance of foot holes
In wet weather, the umpires shall ensure that the holes made by the bowlers and batsmen are cleaned out and dried whenever necessary to facilitate play. In matches of 2 or more days' duration, the umpires shall allow, if necessary, the re-turfing of foot holes made by the bowler in his delivery stride, or the use of quick-setting fillings for the same purpose, before the start of each day's play.

7. Securing of footholds and maintenance of pitch
During play, the umpires shall allow either batsman to beat the pitch with his bat and players to secure their footholds by the use of sawdust, provided that no damage to the pitch is so caused, and Law 42 (Unfair play) is not contravened.

Notes
a Non-turf pitches: *the above Law 10 applies to turf pitches.*

The game is played on non-turf pitches in many countries at various levels. Whilst the conduct of the game on these surfaces should always be in accordance with the Laws of cricket, it is recognised that it may sometimes be necessary for governing bodies to lay down special playing conditions to suit the type of non-turf pitch used in their country.

In matches played against touring teams, any special playing conditions should be agreed in advance by both parties.

b Mowing of the outfield in a match of 2 or more days' duration: *if, for reasons other than ground and weather conditions, daily and complete mowing is not possible, the ground authority shall notify the captains and umpires, before the toss for innings, of the procedure to be adopted for such mowing during the match.*

c Choice of roller: *if there is more than one roller available the captain of the batting side shall have a choice.*

Law 11 – covering the pitch

1. Before the start of a match
Before the start of a match complete covering of the pitch shall be allowed.

15

2. During a match

The pitch shall not be completely covered during a match unless prior arrangement or regulations so provide.

3. Covering bowlers' run-up

Whenever possible, the bowlers' run-up shall be covered, but the covers so used shall not extend further than 4 ft/1.22 m in front of the popping crease.

Notes

a Removal of covers: *the covers should be removed as promptly as possible whenever the weather permits.*

Comments

It should be noted that many competitions have special regulations governing the covering of both the pitch and the bowlers' run-up with regard to distance and period of time.

The covers used for the bowlers' run-up are usually about 18 ft/5.49 m long of which only 4 ft/1.22 m projects on to the pitch in front of the popping crease.

Law 12 – innings

1. Number of innings

A match shall be of one or two innings of each side according to agreement reached before the start of play.

2. Alternate innings

In a two-innings match each side shall take their innings alternately except in the case provided for in Law 13 (The follow-on).

3. The toss

The captains shall toss for the choice of innings on the field of play not later than 15 minutes before the time scheduled for the match to start, or before the time agreed upon for play to start.

4. Choice of innings

The winner of the toss shall notify his decision to bat or to field to the opposing captain not later than 10 minutes before the time scheduled for the match to start, or before the time agreed upon for play to start. The decision shall not thereafter be altered.

5. Continuation after one innings of each side

Despite the terms of **1** above, in a one-innings match, when a result has been reached on the first innings the captains may agree to the continuation of play if, in their opinion, there is a prospect of carrying the game to a further issue in the time left. *See* Law 21 (Result).

Notes

a Limited innings – one-innings match: *in a one-innings match, each innings may, by agreement, be limited by a number of overs or by a period of time.*

b Limited innings – two-innings match: *in a two-innings match, the first innings of each side may, by agreement, be limited to a number of overs or by a period of time.*

Comments

In half-day cricket, it is often agreed to fix a maximum period for an innings. This can be done by limiting an innings to a stated number of 'overs' (*see* Law 17). Law 12.3 is very important: the toss can take place at any time, but the winner can delay his decision to bat or field until 10 minutes before play is due to start.

Law 13 – the follow-on

1. Lead on first innings
In a two-innings match the side which bats first and leads by 200 runs in a match of five days or more, by 150 runs in a three-day or four-day match, by 100 runs in a two-day match, or by 75 runs in a one-day match, shall have the option of requiring the other side to follow their innings.

2. Day's play lost
If no play takes place on the first day of a match of 2 or more day's duration, **1** above shall apply in accordance with the number of days' play remaining from the actual start of the match.

Law 14 – declarations

1. Time of declaration
The captain of the batting side may declare an innings closed at any time during a match irrespective of its duration.

2. Forfeiture of second innings
A captain may forfeit his second innings, provided his decision to do so is notified to the opposing captain and umpires in sufficient time to allow 7 minutes rolling of the pitch. *See* Law 10 (Rolling, sweeping, mowing, watering the pitch and re-marking of creases). The normal 10 minute interval between innings shall be applied.

Law 15 – start of play

1. Call of 'Play'
At the start of each innings and of each day's play and on the resumption of play after any interval or interruption the umpire at the bowler's end shall call 'Play'.

2. Practice on the field
At no time on any day of the match shall there be any bowling or batting practice on the pitch.

No practice may take place on the field if, in the opinion of the umpires, it could result in a waste of time.

3. Trial run-up
No bowler shall have a trial run-up after 'Play' has been called in any session of play, except at the fall of a wicket when an umpire may allow such a trial run-up if he is satisfied that it will not cause any waste of time.

Law 16 – intervals

1. Length
The umpire shall allow such intervals as have been agreed upon for meals, and 10 minutes between each innings.

2. Luncheon interval – innings ending or stoppage within 10 minutes of interval
If an innings ends or there is a stoppage caused by weather or bad light within 10 minutes of the agreed time for the luncheon interval, the interval shall be taken immediately.

The time remaining in the session of play shall be added to the agreed length of the interval but no extra allowance shall be made for the 10 minutes interval between innings.

3. Tea interval – innings ending or stoppage within 30 minutes of interval
If an innings ends or there is a stoppage caused by weather or bad light within 30 minutes of the agreed time for the tea

interval, the interval shall be taken immediately. The interval shall be of the agreed length and, if applicable, shall include the 10 minute interval between innings.

4. Tea interval – continuation of play
If at the agreed time for the tea interval, 9 wickets are down, play shall continue for a period not exceeding 30 minutes or until the innings is concluded.

5. Tea interval – agreement to forego
At any time during the match, the captains may agree to forego a tea interval.

6. Intervals for drinks
If both captains agree before the start of a match that intervals for drinks may be taken, the option to take such intervals shall be available to either side. These intervals shall be restricted to one per session, shall be kept as short as possible, shall not be taken in the last hour of the match and in any case shall not exceed 5 minutes.

The agreed times for these intervals shall be strictly adhered to except that if a wicket falls within 5 minutes of the

agreed time then drinks shall be taken out immediately.

If an innings ends or there is a stoppage caused by weather or bad light within 30 minutes of the agreed time for a drinks interval, there will be no interval for drinks in that session.

At any time during the match the captains may agree to forego any such drinks interval.

Notes
a Tea interval – one-day match: *in a one-day match, a specific time for the tea interval need not necessarily be arranged, and it may be agreed to take this interval between the innings of a one-innings match.*
b Changing the agreed time of intervals: *in the event of the ground, weather or light conditions causing a suspension of play, the umpires, after consultation with the captains, may decide in the interests of time-saving, to bring forward the time of the luncheon or tea interval.*

Law 17 – cessation of play

1. Call of 'Time'
The umpire at the bowler's end shall call 'Time' on the cessation of play before

any interval or interruption of play, at the end of each day's play, and at the conclusion of the match. *See* Law 27 (Appeals).

2. Removal of bails
After the call of 'Time', the umpires shall remove the bails from both wickets.

3. Starting a last over
The last over before an interval or the close of play shall be started provided the umpire, after walking at his normal pace, has arrived at his position behind the stumps at the bowler's end before time has been reached.

4. Completion of the last over of a session
The last over before an interval or the close of play shall be completed unless a batsman is out or retired during that over within 2 minutes of the interval or the close of play or unless the players have occasion to leave the field.

5. Completion of the last over of a match
An over in progress at the close of play on the final day of a match shall be com-

pleted at the request of either captain even if a wicket falls after time has been reached.

If during the last over the players have occasion to leave the field the umpires shall call 'Time' and there shall be no resumption of play and the match shall be at an end.

6. Last hour of match – number of overs

The umpires shall indicate when one hour of playing time of the match remains according to the agreed hours of play. The next over after that moment shall be the first of a minimum of 20 6-ball overs, provided a result is not reached earlier or there is no interval or interruption of play.

7. Last hour of match – intervals between innings and interruptions

If, at the commencement of the last hour of the match, an interval or interruption of play is in progress or if, during the last hour there is an interval between innings or an interruption of play, the minimum number of overs to be bowled on the resumption of play shall be reduced in proportion to the duration, within the last hour of the match, of any such interval or interruption.

The minimum number of overs to be bowled after a resumption of play shall be calculated as follows.

a In the case of an interval or interruption of play being in progress at the commencement of the last hour of the match, or in the case of a first interval or interruption a deduction shall be made from the minimum of 20 6-ball overs.

b If there is a later interval or interruption a further deduction shall be made from the minimum number of overs which should have been bowled following the last resumption of play.

c These deductions shall be based on the following factors.

(i) the number of overs already bowled in the last hour of the match or, in the case of a later interval or interruption in the last session of play

(ii) the number of overs lost as a result of the interval or interruption allowing one 6-ball over for every full three minutes of interval or interruption

(iii) any over left uncompleted at the end of an innings to be excluded from these calculations

(iv) any over of the minimum number to be played which is left uncompleted at the start of an interruption of play shall be completed when play is resumed and to count as one over bowled

(v) an interval to start with the end of an innings and to end 10 minutes later; an interruption to start on the call of 'Time' and to end on the call of 'Play'.

d In the event of an innings being completed and a new innings commencing during the last hour of the match, the number of overs to be bowled in the new innings shall be calculated on the basis of one 6-ball over for every three minutes or part thereof remaining for play; or alternatively on the basis that sufficient overs be bowled to enable the full minimum quota of overs to be completed under circumstances governed by **a**, **b** and **c** above. In all such cases the alternative which allows the greater number of overs shall be employed.

8. Bowler unable to complete an over during last hour of the match

If, for any reason, a bowler is unable to complete an over during the period of play referred to in **6** above, Law 22.7

(Bowler incapacitated or suspended during an over) shall apply.

Law 18 – scoring

1. A run
The score shall be reckoned by runs. A run is scored:

a so often as the batsmen, after a hit or at any time while the ball is in play, shall have crossed and made good their ground from end to end

b when a boundary is scored. *See* Law 19 (Boundaries)

c when penalty runs are awarded. *See* **6** below.

2. Short runs
a If either batsman runs a short run, the umpire shall call and signal 'One short' as soon as the ball becomes dead and that run shall not be scored. A run is short if a batsman fails to make good his ground on turning for a further run.

b Although a short run shortens the succeeding one, the latter, if completed, shall count.

c If either or both batsmen deliberately run short the umpire shall, as soon as he sees that the fielding side have no chance of dismissing either batsman, call and signal 'Dead ball' and disallow any runs attempted or previously scored. The batsmen shall return to their original ends.

d If both batsmen run short in one and the same run, only one run shall be deducted.

e Only if three or more runs are attempted can more than one be short and then, subject to **c** and **d** above, all runs so called shall be disallowed. If there has been more than one short run the umpires shall instruct the scorers as to the number of runs disallowed.

3. Striker caught
If the striker is caught, no run shall be scored.

4. Batsman run out
If a batsman is run out, only that run which was being attempted shall not be scored. If, however, an injured striker himself is run out no runs shall be scored. *See* Law 2.7 (Transgression of the Laws by an injured batsman or runner).

5. Batsman obstructing the field
If a batsman is out obstructing the field, any runs completed before the obstruction occurs shall be scored unless such obstruction prevents a catch being made in which case no runs shall be scored.

6. Runs scored for penalties
Runs shall be scored for penalties under Laws 20 (Lost ball), 24 (No ball), 25 (Wide ball), 41.1 (Fielding the ball) and for boundary allowances under Law 19 (Boundaries).

7. Batsman returning
to wicket he has left
If, while the ball is in play, the batsmen have crossed in running, neither shall return to the wicket he has left even though a short run has been called or no run has been scored as in the case of a catch. Batsmen, however, shall return to the wickets they originally left in the cases of a boundary and of any disallowance of runs and of an injured batsman being, himself, run out. *See* Law 2.7 (Transgression of the Laws by an injured batsman or runner).

Notes

a Short run: *a striker taking stance in front of his popping crease may run from that point without penalty.*

Comments

In spite of the fact that no runs can be scored if the striker is out 'caught', the non-striker remains at the end he has reached if any runs have been attempted. In the case of a 'run out' all completed runs count to the batsmen, except that in which the 'run out' occurred, which of course is not a 'completed' run.

Particular attention is called to Law 18.2 in regard to the failure of both batsmen to make good their ground in one and the same run.

Law 19 – boundaries

1. The boundary of the playing area

Before the toss for innings, the umpires shall agree with both captains on the boundary of the playing area. The boundary shall, if possible, be marked by a white line, a rope laid on the ground, or a fence. If flags or posts only are used to mark a boundary, the imaginary line joining such points shall be regarded as the boundary. An obstacle, or person, within the playing area shall not be regarded as a boundary unless so decided by the umpires before the toss for innings. Sight-screens within, or partially within, the playing area shall be regarded as the boundary and when the ball strikes or passes within or under or directly over any parts of the screen, a boundary shall be scored.

2. Runs scored for boundaries

Before the toss for innings, the umpires shall agree with both captains the runs to be allowed for boundaries, and in deciding the allowance for them, the umpires and captains shall be guided by the prevailing custom of the ground. The allowance for a boundary shall normally be 4 runs, and 6 runs for all hits pitching over and clear of the boundary line or fence, even though the ball has been previously touched by a fieldsman. 6 runs shall also be scored if a fieldsman, after catching a ball, carries it over the boundary. *See* Law 32 (Caught) *Note* **a**. 6 runs shall not be scored when a ball struck by the striker hits a sight-screen full pitch if the screen is within, or partially within, the playing area, but if the ball is struck directly over a sight-screen so situated, 6 runs shall be scored.

3. A boundary

A boundary shall be scored and signalled by the umpire at the bowler's end whenever, in his opinion:

a a ball in play touches or crosses the boundary, however marked

b a fieldsman with ball in hand touches or grounds any part of his person on or over a boundary line

c a fieldsman with ball in hand grounds any part of his person over a boundary fence or board. This allows the fieldsman to touch or lean on or over a boundary fence or board in preventing a boundary.

4. Runs exceeding boundary allowance

The runs completed at the instant the ball reaches the boundary shall count if they exceed the boundary allowance.

5. Overthrows or wilful act of a fieldsman

If the boundary results from an overthrow or from the wilful act of a fieldsman, any runs already completed and the allowance shall be added to the score. The run in progress shall count provided that the batsmen have crossed at the instant of the throw or act.

Notes
a Position of sight-screens: *sight-screens should, if possible, be positioned wholly outside the playing area, as near as possible to the boundary line.*

Comments
It should be noted that if the ball is stopped by any of the obstructions (not being agreed as boundaries) mentioned in Law 19, it remains in play, and a batsman can still be 'run out'.

The fixing of boundaries usually follows the custom of the ground, and the allowances mentioned in Law 19.2 are now commonly accepted.

There is nothing in the Laws or Notes to say that a fieldsman must stop a ball from passing over a boundary, but he may not procure that event by a deliberate act, e.g. by kicking the ball, in order to gain any advantage such as preventing the batsmen crossing.

Law 20 – lost ball

1. Runs scored
If a ball in play cannot be found or recovered any fieldsman may call 'Lost ball' when 6 runs shall be added to the score; but if more than 6 have been run before 'Lost ball' is called, as many runs as have been completed shall be scored. The run in progress shall count provided that the batsmen have crossed at the instant of the call of 'Lost ball'.

2. How scored
The runs shall be added to the score of the striker if the ball has been struck, but otherwise the score of byes, leg-byes, no balls or wides as the case may be.

Comments
The introduction of boundaries and the improvement of outfields have rendered this Law almost redundant. It should be noted, however, that the term 'lost' is used in the sense of temporarily irrecoverable, which can occur when, for example, the ball is lodged on or in an obstruction in the playing area, or has been appropriated by a dog.

It is, of course, perfectly permissible for a fieldsman to call 'Lost ball' well in advance of the batsmen completing 6 runs in order to restrict the liability to that number, but once called, the ball is 'dead' and the penalty is final.

Law 21 – the result

1. A win – two-innings matches
The side which has scored a total of runs in excess of that scored by the opposing side in its two completed innings shall be the winners.

2. A win – one-innings matches
a One-innings matches, unless played out as in **1** above, shall be decided on the first innings, but *see* Law 12.5 (Continuation after one innings of each side).
b If the captains agree to continue play after the completion of one innings of each side in accordance with Law 12.5 (Continuation after one innings of each side) and a result is not achieved on the second innings, the first innings result shall stand.

3. Umpires awarding a match

a A match shall be lost by a side which, during the match,

(i) refuses to play, or

(ii) concedes defeat,

and the umpires shall award the match to the other side.

b Should both batsmen at the wickets or the fielding side leave the field at any time without the agreement of the umpires, this shall constitute a refusal to play and, on appeal, the umpires shall award the match to the other side in accordance with **a** above.

4. A tie

The result of a match shall be a tie when the scores are equal at the conclusion of play, but only if the side batting last has completed its innings.

If the scores of the completed first innings of a one-day match are equal, it shall be a tie but only if the match has not been played out to a further conclusion.

5. A draw

A match not determined in any of the ways as in **1**, **2**, **3** and **4** above shall count as a draw.

6. Correctness of result

Any decision as to the correctness of the scores shall be the responsibility of the umpires. *See* Law 3.14 (Correctness of scores).

If, after the umpires and players have left the field, in the belief that the match has been concluded, the umpires decide that a mistake in scoring has occurred, which affects the result, and provided time has not been reached, they shall order play to resume and to continue until the agreed finishing time unless a result is reached earlier.

If the umpires decide that a mistake has occurred and time has been reached, the umpires shall immediately inform both captains of the necessary corrections to the scores and, if applicable, to the result.

7. Acceptance of result

In accepting the scores as notified by the scorers and agreed by the umpires, the captains of both sides thereby accept the result.

Notes

a Statement of results: *the result of a finished match is stated as a win by runs,* *except in the case of a win by the side batting last when it is by the number of wickets still then to fall.*

b Winning hit or extras: *as soon as the side has won, see 1 and 2 above, the umpire shall call 'Time', the match is finished, and nothing that happens thereafter other than as a result of a mistake in scoring, see 6 above, shall be regarded as part of the match.*

However, if a boundary constitutes the winning hit – or extras – and the boundary allowance exceeds the number of runs required to win the match, such runs scored shall be credited to the side's total and, in the case of a hit, to the striker's score.

Comments

Disputes over the results of matches due to scoring mistakes being discovered too late to correct, are far too frequent. They should not occur if the instructions given in Law 4 and in the notes for scorers and umpires on pages 5–8 are followed. If the umpires are satisfied that a mistake in scoring has occurred, they may, provided time has not been reached, order play to be resumed, or they may award the match against the side which by its acquiescence in the assumed result has 'given up'. In one-day cricket the umpires should always encourage the players to attempt a two-innings conclusion if there is the least chance of this.

As soon as a side has won, the match is finished and nothing that happens afterwards can technically be regarded as part of the play. If the scores are even when, for example, the side batting last has lost 7 wickets and a batsman is run out attempting a second run, or a batsman is 'out' off a no ball, the correct result is that the batting side has won by 3 wickets, as in one case the first run counts, and in the second the penalty for a no ball is not cancelled.

A 'tie' cannot occur in an uncompleted match, e.g. side A, 1st innings 100, 2nd 200; side B, 1st innings 200, 2nd 100 for 5 does not represent a completed match and the result is not a 'tie'.

Law 22 – the over

1. Number of balls
The ball shall be bowled from each wicket alternately in overs of 6 balls.

2. Call of 'Over'
When the number of balls has been bowled, and as the ball becomes dead or when it becomes clear to the umpire at the bowler's end that both the fielding side and the batsmen at the wicket have ceased to regard the ball as in play, the umpire shall call 'Over' before leaving the wicket.

3. No ball or wide ball
Neither a no ball nor a wide ball shall be reckoned as one of the over.

4. Umpire miscounting
If an umpire miscounts the number of balls, the over as counted by the umpire shall stand.

5. Bowler changing ends
A bowler shall be allowed to change ends as often as desired provided only that he does not bowl two overs consecutively in an innings.

6. The bowler finishing an over
A bowler shall finish an over in progress unless he be incapacitated or be suspended under Law 42.8 (The bowling of fast short pitched balls), 42.9 (The

bowling of fast high full pitches), 42.10 (Time wasting) and 42.11 (Players damaging the pitch). If an over is left incomplete for any reason at the start of an interval or interruption of play, it shall be finished on the resumption of play.

7. Bowler incapacitated or suspended during an over
If, for any reason, a bowler is incapacitated while running up to bowl the first ball of an over, or is incapacitated or suspended during an over, the umpire shall call and signal 'Dead ball' and another bowler shall be allowed to bowl or complete the over from the same end, provided only that he shall not bowl two overs, or part thereof, consecutively in one innings.

8. Position of non-striker
The batsman at the bowler's end shall normally stand on the opposite side of the wicket to that from which the ball is being delivered, unless a request to do otherwise is granted by the umpire.

Comments
If an umpire miscounts the number of

balls, any additional balls are valid. This mistake can be avoided if both umpires count and exchange signal (such as spreading five fingers on the trouser pocket) after the fifth ball has become dead.

The umpire should call 'Dead ball' should a bowler be incapacitated while running up to deliver the first ball of an over. The clause of Law 23.3 does not apply in these special circumstances, and another bowler should be deputed to bowl an over from the same end.

Law 23 – dead ball

1. The ball becomes dead, when:
a it is finally settled in the hands of the wicket-keeper or the bowler
b it reaches or pitches over the boundary
c a batsman is out
d whether played or not, it lodges in the clothing or equipment of a batsman or the clothing of an umpire
e it lodges in a protective helmet worn by a member of the fielding side
f a penalty is awarded under Law 20 (Lost ball) or Law 41.1 (Fielding the ball)

g the umpire calls 'Over' or 'Time'.

2. Either umpire shall call and signal 'Dead ball', when:
a he intervenes in a case of unfair play
b a serious injury to a player or umpire occurs
c he is satisfied that, for an adequate reason, the striker is not ready to receive the ball and makes no attempt to play it
d the bowler drops the ball accidentally before delivery, or the ball does not leave his hand for any reason other than in an attempt to run out the non-striker – *see* Law 24.5 (Bowler attempting to run-out non-striker before delivery)
e one or both bails fall from the striker's wicket before he receives delivery
f he leaves his normal position for consultation
g he is required to do so under Law 26.3 (Disallowance of leg-byes), etc.

3. The ball ceases to be dead, when:
a the bowler starts his run up or bowling action.

4. The ball is not dead, when:
a it strikes an umpire (unless it lodges in his dress)

b the wicket is broken or struck down (unless a batsman is out thereby)
c an unsuccessful appeal is made
d the wicket is broken accidentally either by the bowler during his delivery or by a batsman in running
e the umpire has called 'No ball' or 'Wide'.

Notes
a Ball finally settled: *whether the ball is finally settled or not – see **1 a** above – must be a question for the umpires alone to decide.*
b Action on call of 'Dead ball':
(i) *if 'Dead ball' is called prior to the striker receiving a delivery the bowler shall be allowed an additional ball*
(ii) *if 'Dead ball' is called after the striker receives a delivery the bowler shall not be allowed an additional ball, unless 'No ball' or 'Wide' has been called.*

Comments
Umpires should not regard the ball as 'finally settled' and therefore 'dead' if either batsman is 'out of his ground', or if there is any reason to think it may be to the advantage of the fielding side for the ball to remain in play.

Law 24 – no ball

1. Mode of delivery

The umpire shall indicate to the striker whether the bowler intends to bowl over or round the wicket, overarm or underarm, or right or left-handed. Failure on the part of the bowler to indicate in advance a change in his mode of delivery is unfair and the umpire shall call and signal 'No ball'.

2. Fair delivery – the arm

For a delivery to be fair the ball must be bowled not thrown – *see Note* **a** below. If either umpire is not entirely satisfied with the absolute fairness of a delivery in this respect he shall call and signal 'No ball' instantly upon delivery.

3. Fair delivery – the feet

The umpire at the bowler's wicket shall call and signal 'No ball' if he is not satisfied that in the delivery stride:
a the bowler's back foot **has landed within and not touching** the return crease or its forward extension or
b some part of the front foot whether grounded or raised was behind the popping crease.

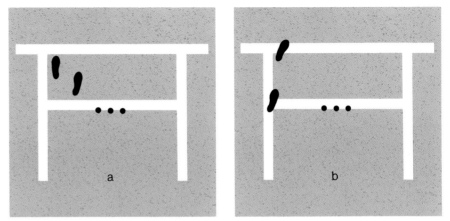

▲ *Fig. 5 The no ball: (a) fair delivery; (b) no ball – back foot is touching return crease; (c) fair delivery; (d) no ball – front foot is over popping crease*

4. Bowler throwing at striker's wicket before delivery

If the bowler, before delivering the ball, throws it at the striker's wicket in an attempt to run him out, the umpire shall call and signal 'No ball '. *See* Law 42.12 (Batsman unfairly stealing a run) and Law 38 (Run out).

5. Bowler attempting to run out non-striker before delivery

If the bowler, before delivering the ball, attempts to run out the non-striker, any runs which result shall be allowed and shall be scored as no balls. Such an attempt shall not count as a ball in the over. The umpire shall not call 'No ball'. *See* Law 42.12 (Batsman unfairly stealing a run).

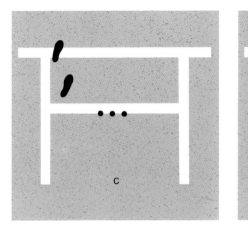

c

d

6. Infringement of laws by a wicket-keeper or a fieldsman
The umpire shall call and signal 'No ball' in the event of the wicket-keeper infringing Law 40.1 (Position of wicket-keeper) or a fieldsman infringing Law 41.2 (Limitation of on-side fieldsmen) or Law 41.3 (Position of fieldsmen).

7. Revoking a call
An umpire shall revoke the call 'No ball' if the ball does not leave the bowler's hand for any reason. *See* Law 23.2 (Either umpire shall call and signal 'Dead ball').

8. Penalty
A penalty of one run for a no ball shall be scored if no runs are made otherwise.

9. Runs from a no ball
The striker may hit a no ball and whatever runs result shall be added to his score. Runs made otherwise from a no ball shall be scored no balls.

10. Out from a no ball
The striker shall be out from a no ball if he breaks Law 34 (Hit the ball twice) and either batsman may be run out or shall be given out if either breaks Law 33 (Handled the ball) or Law 37 (Obstructing the field).

11. Batsman given out off a no ball
Should a batsman be given out off a no ball the penalty for bowling it shall stand unless runs are otherwise scored.

Notes
a Definition of a throw: *a ball shall be deemed to have been thrown if, in the opinion of either umpire, the process of straightening the bowling arm, whether it be partial or complete, takes place during that part of the delivery swing which directly precedes the ball leaving the hand. This definition shall not debar a bowler from the use of the wrist in the delivery swing.*
b No ball not counting in over: *a no ball shall not be reckoned as one of the over.* See *Law 22.3 (No ball or wide ball).*

Comments
If the batsmen do not run for a 'no ball' the penalty of one run is credited under

27

extras. If, however, the ball goes to the boundary, or the batsmen run, the actual number of completed runs are entered, but not the penalty in addition. If the striker has not played the 'no ball' with his bat, such runs are credited under extras; if he has touched it, they are credited to his score. It should be noted that if a batsman is out off a 'no ball' this does not cancel it, and the penalty or runs completed are still credited to the score.

Law 25 – wide ball

1. Judging a wide
If the bowler bowls the ball so high over or so wide of the wicket that, in the opinion of the umpire it passes out of reach of the striker, standing in a normal guard position, the umpire shall call and signal 'Wide ball' as soon as it has passed the line of the striker's wicket.

The umpire shall not adjudge a ball as being a wide if:
a the striker, by moving from his guard position, causes the ball to pass out of his reach
b the striker moves and thus brings the ball within his reach.

2. Penalty
A penalty of one run for a wide shall be scored if no runs are made otherwise.

3. Ball coming to rest in front of the striker
If a ball which the umpire considers to have been delivered comes to rest in front of the line of the striker's wicket, 'Wide' shall not be called. The striker has a right, without interference from the fielding side, to make one attempt to hit the ball. If the fielding side interfere, the umpire shall replace the ball where it came to rest and shall order the fieldsmen to resume the places they occupied in the field before the ball was delivered.

The umpire shall call and signal 'Dead ball' as soon as it is clear that the striker does not intend to hit the ball, or after the striker has made one unsuccessful attempt to hit the ball.

4. Revoking a call
The umpire shall revoke the call if the striker hits a ball which has been called 'Wide'.

5. Ball not dead
The ball does not become dead on the call of 'Wide ball' – see Law 23.4 (The ball is not dead).

6. Runs resulting from a wide
All runs which are run or result from a wide ball which is not a no ball shall be scored wide balls, or if no runs are made one shall be scored.

7. Out from a wide
The striker shall be out from a wide ball if he breaks Law 35 (Hit wicket) or Law 39 (Stumped). Either batsman may be run out and shall be out if he breaks Law 33 (Handled the ball) or Law 37 (Obstructing the field).

8. Batsman given out off a wide
Should a batsman be given out off a wide, the penalty for bowling it shall stand unless runs are otherwise made.

Notes
a Wide ball not counting in over: *a wide ball shall not be reckoned as one of the over – see Law 22.3 (No ball or wide ball).*

Comments

A 'no ball' by definition is not a properly delivered ball and cannot therefore be a 'wide' in addition.

It should be noted that· 'wides' can never be credited to the striker's score since if the ball is struck the call of 'wide' should be revoked. (*See* Law 25.4.)

The fact that a batsman may be given out off a 'wide' does not affect the penalty for bowling it, so that the penalty or any runs actually completed while the ball remains in play are credited to the batting side.

As in the case of a 'no ball', if a 'wide' goes to the boundary or the batsmen run, the actual boundary allowance or number of completed runs is entered as 'wides' under extras.

Law 26 – bye and leg-bye

1. Byes

If the ball, not having been called 'Wide' or 'No ball', passes the striker without touching his bat or person, and any runs are obtained, the umpire shall signal 'bye' and the run or runs shall be credited as such to the batting side.

2. Leg-byes

If the ball, not having been called 'Wide' or 'No ball', is unintentionally deflected by the striker's dress or person, except a hand holding the bat, and any runs are obtained the umpire shall signal 'leg-bye' and the run or runs so scored shall be credited as such to the batting side.

Such leg-byes shall only be scored if, in the opinion of the umpire, the striker has:

a attempted to play the ball with his bat, or

b tried to avoid being hit by the ball.

3. Disallowance of leg-byes

In the case of a deflection by the striker's person, other than in **2a** and **b** above, the umpire shall call and signal 'Dead ball' as soon as one run has been completed or when it is clear that a run is not being attempted or the ball has reached the boundary.

On the call and signal of 'Dead ball' the batsmen shall return to their original ends and no runs shall be allowed.

Law 27 – appeals

1. Time of appeals

The umpires shall not give a batsman out unless appealed to by the other side which shall be done prior to the bowler beginning his run-up or bowling action to deliver the next ball. Under Law 23.1 **g** (The ball becomes dead) the ball is dead on 'Over' being called; this does not, however, invalidate an appeal made prior to the first ball of the following over provided 'Time' has not been called. *See* Law 17.1 (Call of 'Time').

2. An appeal 'How's that?'

An appeal 'How's that?' shall cover all ways of being out.

3. Answering appeals

The umpire at the bowler's wicket shall answer appeals before the other umpire in all cases except those arising out of Law 35 (Hit wicket) or Law 39 (Stumped) or Law 38 (Run out) when this occurs at the striker's wicket.

When either umpire has given a batsman not out, the other umpire shall, within his jurisdiction, answer the appeal or a further appeal, provided it is made in time in accordance with 1 above (Time of appeals).

▲ *An appeal 'How's that?' shall cover all ways of being out. The umpire's decision is final*

▲ *The batsman has been given out. The umpire raises the index finger above the head to signal this*

4. Consultation by umpires
An umpire may consult with the other umpire on a point of fact which the latter may have been in a better position to see and shall then give his decision. If, after consultation, there is still doubt remaining the decision shall be in favour of the batsman.

5. Batsman leaving his wicket under a misapprehension
The umpire shall intervene if satisfied that a batsman, not having been given out, has left his wicket under a misapprehension that he has been dismissed.

6. Umpire's decision

The umpire's decision is final. He may alter his decision, provided that such alteration is made promptly.

7. Withdrawal of an appeal

In exceptional circumstances the captain of the fielding side may seek permission of the umpire to withdraw an appeal providing the outgoing batsman has not left the playing area. If this is allowed, the umpire shall cancel his decision.

Comments

By custom, in many cases where the decision is obvious no appeal is made and the batsmen accept their dismissal.

If an appeal is delayed, and runs are made before a batsman is given out, the umpires should instruct the scorers to disregard any runs to which the batting side are not entitled, e.g. if before the striker is given out L.B.W. the batsmen have run a 'leg-bye', this run should be disallowed and the non-striker should return to his original end.

If the striker is out 'caught', then the position of the non-striker will depend on whether the batsmen had crossed at the instant the catch was made.

Law 27.5, of course, does not protect a batsman who leaves his ground while the ball is in play, e.g. a batsman wrongly expecting a catch to be caught, leaves his ground and as a result is 'run out'.

Law 28 – the wicket is down

1. Wicket down

The wicket is down if:

a either the ball or the striker's bat or person completely removes either bail from the top of the stumps. A disturbance of a bail, whether temporary or not, shall not constitute a complete removal, but the wicket is down if a bail in falling lodges between two of the stumps

b any player completely removes with his hand or arm a bail from the top of the stumps, providing that the ball is held in that hand or in the hand of the arm so used

c when both bails are off, a stump is struck out of the ground by the ball, or a player strikes or pulls a stump out of the ground, providing that the ball is held in the hand(s) or in the hand of the arm so used.

2. One bail off

If one bail is off, it shall be sufficient for the purpose of putting the wicket down to remove the remaining bail, or to strike or pull any of the three stumps out of the ground in any of the ways stated in 1 above.

3. All the stumps out of the ground

If all the stumps are out of the ground, the fielding side shall be allowed to put back one or more stumps in order to have an opportunity of putting the wicket down.

4. Dispensing with bails

If owing to the strength of the wind, it has been agreed to dispense with the bails in accordance with Law 8 *Note* **a** (Dispensing with bails) the decision as to when the wicket is down is one for the umpires to decide on the facts before them. In such circumstances and if the umpires so decide the wicket shall be held to be down even though a stump has not been struck out of the ground.

Notes

a Remaking the wicket: *if the wicket is broken while the ball is in play, it is not the umpire's duty to remake the wicket until the ball has become dead – see Law 23 (Dead ball). A member of the fielding side, however, may remake the wicket in such circumstances.*

Comments

Particular attention is called to Law 28.2. The fact that one bail is already off in no way prevents the wicket being legitimately broken by the removal of the other bail.

Regarding Law 28.1, it will be understood from the Law that even if the bails are off, the wicket can be bowled or thrown down if the ball strikes a stump entirely out of its hole in the ground. Alternatively a player can put down the wicket by pulling up a stump with the hand or hands holding the ball. If all the stumps are on the ground, the fielding side is allowed by Law 28.3 to put back one or more stumps in order to have an opportunity of breaking the wicket.

Under Law 23.2, if either or both bails are blown off the striker's wicket before he received delivery, then the umpire

should call 'Dead ball' and in that case the ball will be cancelled and another bowled in its place.

Law 29 – batsman out of his ground

1. When out of his ground

A batsman shall be considered to be out of his ground unless some part of his bat in his hand or of his person is grounded behind the line of the popping crease.

Law 30 – bowled

1. Out bowled

The striker shall be out bowled if:
a his wicket is bowled down, even if the ball first touches his bat or person
b he breaks his wicket by hitting or kicking the ball on to it before the completion of a stroke, or as a result of attempting to guard his wicket. *See* Law 34.1 (Out – hit the ball twice).

Notes

a Out bowled – not L.B.W.: *the striker is out bowled if the ball is deflected on to his wicket even though a decision against him would be justified under Law 36 (L.B.W.).*

▲ *The batsman's wicket is bowled down*

Comments

The term 'played on' is merely a descriptive one and should not be used in the score sheet.

Law 31 – timed out

1. Out timed out

An incoming batsman shall be out timed out if he wilfully takes more than two minutes to come in – the two minutes being timed from the moment a wicket falls until the new batsman steps on to the field of play.

If this is not complied with and if the umpire is satisfied that the delay was wilful and if an appeal is made, the new batsman shall be given out by the umpire at the bowler's end.

2. Time to be added

The time taken by the umpires to investigate the cause of the delay shall be added at the normal close of play.

Notes

a Entry in score book: *the correct entry in the score book when a batsman is given out under this Law is 'timed out', and the bowler does not get credit for the wicket.*

b Batsmen crossing on the field of play: *it is an essential duty of the captains to ensure that the in-going batsman passes the out-going one before the latter leaves the field of play.*

Law 32 – caught

1. Out caught

The striker shall be out caught if the ball touches his bat or if it touches below the wrist his hand or glove, holding the bat, and is subsequently held by a fieldsman before it touches the ground.

2. A fair catch

A catch shall be considered to have been fairly made if:

a the fieldsman is within the field of play throughout the act of making the catch

(i) the act of making the catch shall start from the time when the fieldsman first handles the ball and shall end when he both retains complete control over the further disposal of the ball and remains within the field of play

(ii) in order to be within the field of play, the fieldsman may not touch or ground any part of his person on or over a boundary line. When the boundary is marked by a fence or board the fieldsman may not ground any part of his person over the boundary fence or board, but may touch or lean over the boundary fence or board in completing the catch

b the ball is hugged to the body of the catcher or accidentally lodges in his dress or, in the case of the wicket-keeper, in his pads. However, a striker may not be caught if a ball lodges in a protective helmet worn by a fieldsman, in which case the umpire shall call and signal 'Dead ball'. *See* Law 23 (Dead ball)

c the ball does not touch the ground even though a hand holding it does so in effecting the catch

d a fieldsman catches the ball, after it has been lawfully played a second time by the striker, but only if the ball has not touched the ground since being first struck

e a fieldsman catches the ball after it has touched an umpire, another fieldsman or the other batsman. However a striker may not be caught if a ball has touched a protective helmet worn by a fieldsman

33

◀ *A catch shall be considered to have been fairly made if the ball does not touch the ground even though a hand holding it does so in effecting the catch*

ball will be considered to be still in play and it may be caught by another fieldsman. However, if the original fieldsman returns to the field of play and handles the ball, a catch may not be made.

Comments

A catch is regarded as 'made' at the instant the fieldsman remaining in the field of play has complete control over the further disposal of the ball. The juggling of a catch ending in the ball being dropped may last a second or two, whereas the effective holding of a 'hot' return may be instantaneous.

Some confusion has arisen amongst players over the ball which first hits the pad and then hits the bat. In this case the striker could be out either caught or L.B.W., depending on the other circumstances.

f the ball is caught off an obstruction within the boundary provided it has not previously been agreed to regard the obstruction as a boundary.

3. Scoring of runs
If a striker is caught, no runs shall be scored.

Notes
a Scoring from an attempted catch: *when a fieldsman carrying the ball touches or grounds any part of his person on or over a boundary marked by a line, 6 runs shall be scored.*
b Ball still in play: *if a fieldsman releases the ball before he crosses the boundary, the*

Note that the striker is not 'caught' if a ball strikes a hand which is no longer holding the handle of the bat, e.g. the striker may have taken a hand off to guard his face against a bouncer.

Law 33 – handled the ball

1. Out handled the ball
Either batsman on appeal shall be out handled the ball if he wilfully touches the ball while in play with the hand not holding the bat unless he does so with the consent of the opposite side.

Notes
a Entry in score book: *the correct entry in the score book when a batsman is given out under this Law is 'handled the ball', and the bowler does not get credit for the wicket.*

Comments
The handling of the ball while it is in play by either batsman should never occur except at the specific request of the fielding side. If it does and there is an appeal, the umpires are bound by the Law to give the offender out. The Law is not intended to apply to an involuntary handling such as a player protecting his face from a bouncer by taking his hand off the bat.

Law 34 – hit the ball twice

1. Out hit the ball twice
The striker, on appeal, shall be out hit the ball twice if, after the ball is struck or is stopped by any part of his person, he wilfully strikes it again with his bat or person except for the sole purpose of guarding his wicket: this he may do with his bat or any part of his person other than his hands, but *see* Law 37.2 (Obstructing a ball from being caught).

For the purpose of this Law, a hand holding the bat shall be regarded as part of the bat.

2. Returning the ball to a fieldsman
The striker, on appeal, shall be out under this Law, if, without the consent of the opposite side, he uses his bat or person to return the ball to any of the fielding side.

3. Runs from ball lawfully struck twice
No runs except those which result from an overthrow or penalty, *see* Law 41 (The fieldsman), shall be scored from a ball lawfully struck twice.

Notes
a Entry in score book: *the correct entry in the score book when the striker is given out under this Law is 'hit the ball twice', and the bowler does not get credit for the wicket.*
b Runs credited to the batsman: *any runs awarded under 3 above as a result of an overthrow or penalty shall be credited to the striker, provided the ball in the first instance has touched the bat, or, if otherwise as extras.*

Comments
Attention is specially drawn to Law 34.2; a batsman should not knock the ball back to the bowler, wicket-keeper or any fieldsman unless specifically asked to do so.

Law 35 – hit wicket

1. Out hit wicket
The striker shall be out hit wicket if, while the ball is in play:
a his wicket is broken with any part of his person, dress, or equipment as a result of any action taken by him in

35

preparing to receive or in receiving a delivery, or in setting off for his first run, immediately after playing, or playing at, the ball

b he hits down his wicket whilst lawfully making a second stroke for the purpose of guarding his wicket within the provisions of Law 34.1 (Out hit the ball twice).

Notes

a Not out hit wicket: *a batsman is not out under this Law should his wicket be broken in any of the ways referred to in* **1a** *above if:*
(i) it occurs while he is in the act of running, other than in setting off for his first run immediately after playing at the ball, or while he is avoiding being run out or stumped
(ii) the bowler after starting his run-up or bowling action does not deliver the ball; in which case the umpire shall immediately call and signal 'Dead ball'
(iii) it occurs whilst he is avoiding a throw-in at any time.

Comments

The chief difficulty in applying this Law is to decide the end of the action of playing at the ball. The words should be interpreted to include any action of the striker's bat or person which occurs from the moment he starts to receive a delivery until the absolute conclusion of his attempt to play the ball – this includes for example the striker's swing round or follow through in playing a ball on the leg side.

Law 36 – Leg Before Wicket

1. Out L.B.W.

The striker shall be out L.B.W. in the circumstances set out below.

a Striker attempting to play the ball
The striker shall be out L.B.W. if he first intercepts with any part of his person, dress or equipment a fair ball which would have hit the wicket and which has not previously touched his bat or a

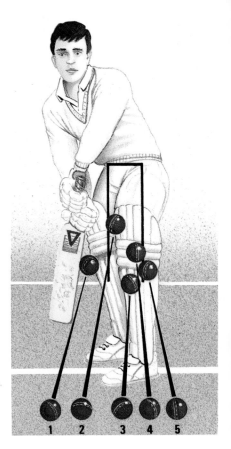

Fig. 6 L.B.W.: (1) not out – ball not ▶ pitching between wicket and wicket and batsman attempting a stroke; (2) and (3) out – if ball not rising to pass over stumps; (4) out – if leg break not enough to make ball pass outside off stump; (5) not out – ball pitching outside line of leg stump

hand holding the bat, provided that:

(i) the ball pitched in a straight line between wicket and wicket or on the off side of the striker's wicket, or was intercepted full pitch, and

(ii) the point of impact is in a straight line between wicket and wicket, even if above the level of the bails.

b Striker making no attempt to play the ball

The striker shall be out L.B.W. even if the ball is intercepted outside the line of the off stump, if, in the opinion of the umpire, he has made no genuine attempt to play the ball with his bat, but has intercepted the ball with some part of his person and if the other circumstances set out in **a** above apply.

Comments

It is fundamental that the striker cannot be out L.B.W. from any ball pitched outside the line of the leg stump, or from one that would pass to either side or over the top of the wicket.

In connection with Law 36 the following are common misconceptions:

a that the umpires must give the striker the benefit of any doubt

b that bowlers who bowl round the wicket cannot ever succeed in appeals for L.B.W.

c that a striker who touches the ball with his bat before it strikes his person can be out L.B.W.

When a striker in playing forward is hit full pitch the umpire should be careful in deciding whether the ball would have hit the wicket or not: the chance of this may be small in the case of a ball which is swinging.

Law 37 – obstructing the field

1. Wilful obstruction

Either batsman, on appeal, shall be out obstructing the field if he wilfully obstructs the opposite side by word or action.

2. Obstructing a ball from being caught

The striker, on appeal, shall be out should wilful obstruction by either batsman prevent a catch being made.

This shall apply even though the striker causes the obstruction in lawfully guarding his wicket under the provisions of Law 34. *See* Law 34.1 (Out hit the ball twice).

Notes

a Accidental obstruction: *the umpires must decide whether the obstruction was wilful or not. The accidental interception of a throw-in by a batsman while running does not break this Law.*

b Entry in score book: *the correct entry in the score book when a batsman is given out under this Law is 'obstructing the field', and the bowler does not get credit for the wicket.*

Law 38 – run out

1. Out run out

Either batsman shall be out run out if in running or at any time while the ball is in play – except in the circumstances described in Law 39 (Stumped) – he is out of his ground and his wicket is put down by the opposite side. If, however, a batsman in running makes good his ground he shall not be out run out, if he subsequently leaves his ground, in order to avoid injury, and the wicket is put down.

2. 'No ball' called

If a no ball has been called, the striker shall not be given run out unless he attempts to run.

▲ *The wicket-keeper has put down the wicket. If the umpire deems that the batsman, in running while the ball is in play, is out of his ground, the batsman is run out*

man remains in his ground or returns to his ground and the other batsman joins him there, the latter shall be out if his wicket is put down.

4. Scoring of runs

If a batsman is run out, only that run which is being attempted shall not be scored. If however an injured striker himself is run out, no runs shall be scored. *See* Law 2.7 (Transgression of the Laws by an injured batsman or runner).

Notes

a Ball played on to opposite wicket: *if the ball is played on to the opposite wicket neither batsman is liable to be run out unless the ball has been touched by a fieldsman before the wicket is broken.*

b Entry in score book: *the correct entry in the score book when the striker is given out under this Law is 'run out', and the bowler does not get credit for the wicket.*

c Run out off a fieldsman's helmet: *if, having been played by a batsman, or having come off his person, the ball rebounds directly from the fieldsman's helmet on to the stumps, with either batsman out of his ground, the batsman shall be not out.*

3. Which batsman is out

If the batsmen have crossed in running, he who runs for the wicket which is put down shall be out; if they have not crossed, he who has left the wicket which is put down shall be out. If a bats-

Comments

It is clear from Laws 38 and 39.2 that an appeal for 'stumped' can only be justified if the wicket has been put down by the wicket-keeper without the ball being touched by any other fieldsman, and is limited by Law 39.1 to the actual time of the striker receiving the ball. All other cases of appeals when a wicket is put down with a batsman out of his ground must come under Law 38, i.e. 'run out'.

The striker can never be stumped off a 'no ball' (*see* Law 39.1) nor can he be run out unless he is attempting a run.

If a batsman remains in his ground and the other batsman joins him there, it is the latter who is run out if the farther wicket is put down.

Law 39 – stumped

1. Out stumped

The striker shall be out stumped if, in receiving a ball, not being a no ball, he is out of his ground otherwise than in attempting a run and the wicket is put down by the wicket-keeper without the intervention of another fieldsman.

2. Action by the wicket-keeper

The wicket-keeper may take the ball in front of the wicket in an attempt to stump the striker only if the ball has touched the bat or person of the striker.

▲ *An attempted stumping by the wicket-keeper. If the umpire deems that the batsman, in receiving a ball, is out of his ground, the batsman is given out stumped*

Notes

a Ball rebounding from wicket-keeper's person: *the striker may be out stumped if in the circumstances stated in **1** above, the wicket is broken by a ball rebounding from the wicket-keeper's person or equipment other than a protective helmet or is kicked or thrown by the wicket-keeper on to the wicket.*

Law 40 – the wicket-keeper

1. Position of wicket-keeper

The wicket-keeper shall remain wholly behind the wicket until a ball delivered by the bowler touches the bat or person of the striker, or passes the wicket, or until the striker attempts a run.

In the event of the wicket-keeper contravening this Law, the umpire at the striker's end shall call and signal 'No ball' at the instant of delivery or as soon as possible thereafter.

2. Restriction on actions of the wicket-keeper

If the wicket-keeper interferes with the striker's right to play the ball and to guard his wicket, the striker shall not be out, except under Laws 33 (Handled the

▲ *Wicket-keeper's gloves*

▼ *Wicket-keeper's legguards*

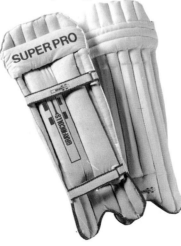

ball), 34 (Hit the ball twice), 37 (Obstructing the field) and 38 (Run out).

3. Interference with the wicket-keeper by the striker

If in the legitimate defence of his wicket, the striker interferes with the wicket-keeper, he shall not be out, except as provided for in Law 37.2 (Obstructing a ball from being caught).

Comments

Law 39.2 clearly states when the wicket-keeper may take the ball in front of the wicket. If the wicket-keeper has taken the ball in front of the wicket, and if the ball has not been touched, he cannot put down the wicket in order to stump the striker.

The wicket-keeper, if standing back, can throw the ball at the wicket or put it down in any of the ways provided in Law 28. Under Law 39 *Note* **a** a ball rebounding off the wicket-keeper's person or equipment (or kicked or thrown by him on to the wicket) also justifies an appeal for stumping.

▲ *The wicket-keeper shall remain wholly behind the wicket until a ball delivered by the bowler touches the bat or person of the striker, or passes the wicket, or until the striker attempts a run. In this instance the striker's wicket has been bowled down*

Law 41 – the fieldsman

1. Fielding the ball

The fieldsman may stop the ball with any part of his person, but if he wilfully stops it otherwise, 5 runs shall be added to the run or runs already scored; if no run has been scored 5 penalty runs shall be awarded. The run in progress shall count provided that the batsmen have crossed at the instant of the act. If the ball has been struck, the penalty shall be added to the score of byes, leg-byes, no balls or wides as the case may be.

2. Limitation of on-side fieldsmen

The number of on-side fieldsmen behind the popping crease at the instant of the bowler's delivery shall not exceed two. In the event of infringement by the fielding side the umpire at the striker's end shall call and signal 'No ball' at the instant of delivery or as soon as possible thereafter.

3. Position of fieldsmen

Whilst the ball is in play and until the ball has made contact with the bat or the striker's person or has passed his bat, no fieldsman, other than the

▲ *A fieldsman may not stand or have any part of his person extended over the pitch whilst the ball is in play and until the ball has made contact with the bat or the striker's person or has passed his bat*

bowler, may stand on or have any part of his person extended over the pitch (measuring 22 yards/20.12 m × 10 ft/ 3.05 m). In the event of a fieldsman contravening this Law, the umpire at the bowler's end shall call and signal 'No ball' at the instant of delivery or as soon as possible thereafter, *See* Law 40.1 (Position of wicket-keeper).

4. Fieldsmen's protective helmets

Protective helmets, when not in use by members of the fielding side, shall only be placed, if above the surface, on the ground behind the wicket-keeper. In the event of the ball, when in play, striking a helmet whilst in this position, 5 penalty runs shall be awarded, as laid down in Law 41.1 and *Note* **a**.

▲ *Protective helmet*

Notes

a Batsmen changing ends: *the 5 runs referred to in* **1** *above are a penalty and the batsmen do not change ends solely by reason of this penalty.*

Law 42 —unfair play

1. Responsibility of captains
The captains are responsible at all times for ensuring that play is conducted within the spirit of the game as well as within the Laws.

2. Responsibility of umpires
The umpires are the sole judges of fair and unfair play.

3. Intervention by the umpire
The umpires shall intervene without appeal by calling and signalling 'Dead ball' in the case of unfair play, but should not otherwise interfere with the progress of the game except as required to do so by the Laws.

4. Lifting the seam
A player shall not lift the seam of the ball for any reason. Should this be done, the umpires shall change the ball for one of similar condition to that in use prior to the contravention. See Note **a**.

5. Changing the condition of the ball
Any member of the fielding side may polish the ball provided that such polishing wastes no time and that no artificial substance is used. No-one shall rub the ball on the ground or use any artificial substance or take any other action to alter the condition of the ball.

In the event of a contravention of this Law, the umpires, after consultation, shall change the ball for one of similar condition to that in use prior to the contravention.

This Law does not prevent a member of the fielding side from drying a wet ball, or removing mud from the ball. See Note **b**.

6. Incommoding the striker
An umpire is justified in intervening under this Law and shall call and signal 'Dead ball' if, in his opinion, any player of the fielding side incommodes the striker by any noise or action while he is receiving a ball.

7. Obstruction of a batsman in running
It shall be considered unfair if any fieldsman wilfully obstructs a batsman in running. In these circumstances the umpire shall call and signal 'Dead ball' and allow any completed runs and the run in progress or alternatively any boundary scored.

8. The bowling of fast short pitched balls
The bowling of fast short pitched balls is unfair if, in the opinion of the umpire at the bowler's end, it constitutes an attempt to intimidate the striker. See Note **d**.

Umpires shall consider intimidation to be the deliberate bowling of fast short pitched balls which by their length, height and direction are intended or likely to inflict physical injury on the striker. The relative skill of the striker shall also be taken into consideration.

In the event of such unfair bowling, the umpire at the bowler's end shall adopt the following procedure.
a In the first instance the umpire shall call and signal 'No ball', caution the bowler and inform the other umpire, the captain of the fielding side and the batsmen of what has occurred.
b If this caution is ineffective, he shall repeat the above procedure and indicate to the bowler that this is a final warning.
c Both the above caution and final

warning shall continue to apply even though the bowler may later change ends.

d Should the above warnings prove ineffective the umpire at the bowler's end shall:

(i) at the first repetition call and signal 'No ball' and when the ball is dead direct the captain to take the bowler off forthwith and to complete the over with another bowler, provided that the bowler does not bowl two overs or part thereof consecutively. *See* Law 22.7 (Bowler incapacitated or suspended during an over)

(ii) not allow the bowler, thus taken off, to bowl again in the same innings

(iii) report the occurrence to the captain of the batting side as soon as the players leave the field for an interval

(iv) report the occurrence to the executive of the fielding side and to any governing body responsible for the match who shall take any further action which is considered to be appropriate against the bowler concerned.

9. The bowling of fast high full pitches

The bowling of fast high full pitches is unfair. *See Note* e. In the event of such unfair bowling the umpire at the bowler's end shall adopt the procedures of caution, final warning, action against the bowler and reporting as set out in **8** above.

10. Time wasting

Any form of time wasting is unfair.

a In the event of the captain of the fielding side wasting time or allowing any member of his side to waste time, the umpire at the bowler's end shall adopt the following procedure.

(i) In the first instance he shall caution the captain of the fielding side and inform the other umpire of what has occurred.

(ii) If this caution is ineffective he shall repeat the above procedure and indicate to the captain that this is a final warning.

(iii) The umpire shall report the occurrence to the captain of the batting side as soon as the players leave the field for an interval.

(iv) Should the above procedure prove ineffective the umpire shall report the occurrence to the executive of the fielding side and to any governing body responsible for that match who shall take appropriate action against the captain and the players concerned.

b In the event of a bowler taking unnecessarily long to bowl an over the umpire at the bowler's end shall adopt the procedures, other than the calling of 'No ball', of caution, final warning, action against the bowler and reporting as set out in **8** above.

c In the event of a batsman wasting time (*see Note* f) other than in the manner described in Law 31 (Timed out), the umpire at the bowler's end shall adopt the following procedure.

(i) In the first instance he shall caution the batsman and inform the other umpire at once, and the captain of the batting side, as soon as the players leave the field for an interval, of what has occurred.

(ii) If this proves ineffective, he shall repeat the caution, indicate to the batsman that this is a final warning and inform the other umpire.

(iii) The umpire shall report the occurrence to both captains as soon as the players leave the field for an interval.

(iv) Should the above procedure prove ineffective, the umpire shall report the occurrence to the executive of the batting side and to any governing body responsible for that match who shall take appropriate action against the player concerned.

11. Players damaging the pitch

The umpires shall intervene and prevent players from causing damage to the pitch which may assist the bowlers of either side. *See Note* c.

a In the event of any member of the fielding side damaging the pitch the umpire shall follow the procedure of caution, final warning and reporting as set out in **10 a** above.

b In the event of a bowler contravening this Law by running down the pitch after delivering the ball, the umpire at the bowler's end shall first caution the bowler. If this caution is ineffective the umpire shall adopt the procedures, other than the calling of 'No ball', of final warning, action against the bowler and reporting as set out in **8** above.

c In the event of a batsman damaging the pitch the umpire at the bowler's end shall follow the procedures of caution, final warning and reporting as set out in **10 c** above.

12. Batsman unfairly stealing a run

Any attempt by the batsman to steal a run during the bowler's run-up is unfair. Unless the bowler attempts to run out either batsman – *see* Law 24.4 (Bowler throwing at striker's wicket before delivery) and Law 24.5 (Bowler attempting to run out non-striker before delivery) – the umpire shall call and signal 'Dead ball' as soon as the batsmen cross in any such attempt to run. The batsmen shall then return to their original wickets.

13. Players' conduct

In the event of a player failing to comply with the instructions of an umpire, criticising his decisions by word or action, or showing dissent, or generally behaving in a manner which might bring the game into disrepute, the umpire concerned shall, in the first place report the matter to the other umpire and to the player's captain requesting the latter to take action. If this proves ineffective, the umpire shall report the incident as soon as possible to the executive of the player's team and to any governing body responsible for the match, who shall take any further

action which is considered appropriate against the player or players concerned.

Notes

a The condition of the ball: *umpires shall make frequent and irregular inspections of the condition of the ball.*

b Drying of a wet ball: *a wet ball may be dried on a towel or with sawdust.*

c Danger area: *the danger area on the pitch, which must be protected from damage by a bowler, shall be regarded by the umpires as the area contained by an imaginary line 4 ft/1.22 m from the popping crease, and parallel to it, and within two imaginary and parallel lines drawn down the pitch from points on that line 1 ft/30.48 cm on either side of the middle stump.*

d Fast short pitched balls: *as a guide, a fast short pitched ball is one which pitches short and passes, or would have passed, above the shoulder height of the striker standing in a normal batting stance at the crease.*

e The bowling of fast full pitches: *the bowling of one fast high full pitch shall be considered to be unfair if, in the opinion of the umpire, it is deliberate, bowled at the striker, and if it passes or would have passed* above the shoulder height of the striker when standing in a normal batting stance at the crease.

f Time wasting by batsmen: *other than in exceptional circumstances, the batsman should always be ready to take strike when the bowler is ready to start his run-up.*

The bowling of fast short pitched balls is ▶ unfair if, in the opinion of the umpire at the bowler's end, it constitutes an attempt to intimidate the striker. Umpires shall consider intimidation to be the deliberate bowling of fast short pitched balls which by their length, height and direction are intended or likely to inflict physical injury on the striker. The relative skill of the striker shall also be taken into consideration. As a guide, a fast short pitched ball is one which pitches short and passes, or would have passed, above the shoulder height of the striker standing in a normal batting stance at the crease.

Index